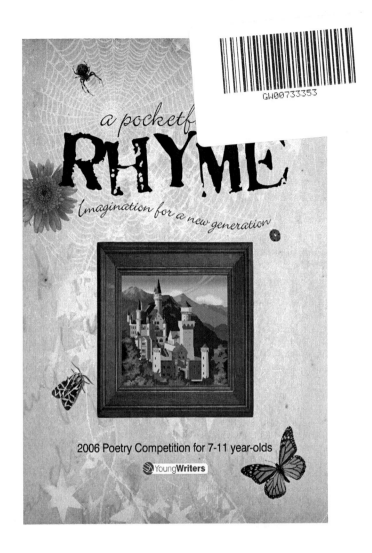

a pocketf

RHYME

Imagination for a new generation

2006 Poetry Competition for 7-11 year-olds

Young**Writers**

London & The Home Counties
Vol II
Edited by Mark Richardson

 Young**Writers**

First published in Great Britain in 2006 by:
Young Writers
Remus House
Coltsfoot Drive
Peterborough
PE2 9JX
Telephone: 01733 890066
Website: www.youngwriters.co.uk

SB ISBN 1 84602 478 1

Foreword

Young Writers was established in 1991 and has been passionately devoted to the promotion of reading and writing in children and young adults ever since. The quest continues today. Young Writers remains as committed to the nurturing of poetic and literary talent as ever.

This year's Young Writers competition has proven as vibrant and dynamic as ever and we are delighted to present a showcase of the best poetry from across the UK and in some cases overseas. Each poem has been selected from a wealth of *A Pocketful Of Rhyme* entries before ultimately being published in this, our fourteenth primary school poetry series.

Once again, we have been supremely impressed by the overall quality of the entries we have received. The imagination, energy and creativity which has gone into each young writer's entry made choosing the poems a challenging and often difficult but ultimately hugely rewarding task - the general high standard of the work submitted ensured this opportunity to bring their poetry to a larger appreciative audience.

We sincerely hope you are pleased with this final collection and that you will enjoy *A Pocketful Of Rhyme London & The Home Counties Vol II* for many years to come.

Contents

Olivia Vine (10)   37
Archie Luckhurst (9)   38
Amy Balmforth (9)   39
Adelle Caines (9)   40

Downsway Primary School, Reading

William Smith (9)   41
Reece Weatherley (9)   42
Alex Winn (9)   43
Bethan Thomas (10)   44
Oliver Smith (9)   45
Toby Herman (9)   46
Amy Hatter (9)   47
Jack Mintern (9)   48
Maisie Pitchford (10)   49
Sarah Lawrence (10)   50
Daniel Holmes (10)   51
Tabitha Grove (9)   52
Jamie Gorman (10)   53
Connor Froude (10)   54
Louella Minter (10)   55
Luke Gracey (9)   56
Andrew Childs (9)   57
Cameron Murgatroyd (9)   58
Connor Almond (9)   59
Lewis Davies (10)   60
Ryan Davey (10)   61
Andrew Allen (9)   62

East Court School for Dyslexia, Ramsgate

Max Keel (9)   63
William Catchpole   64
Jonathon Spurin (11)   65
Oliver Hadman (10)   66
William Colyer (9)   67
Sam Draper (11)   68
Petrok Lawrence (10)   69
Peter Caspell (10)   70
Matthew Pelizzoli (10)   71
Maddie Ford (10)   72
Eve Ricketts (11)   73

Callum McGregor (10)   74
Charles Connell (9)   75
Max Ellison (10)   76
Sean Gilligan (11)   77
Luke Lennard (10)   78

Elsley Primary School, Wembley
Sulakshan Ranaweera (8)   79
Sahra Jama (8)   80
Mohammed Ayyub Khan (8)   81
Noor Salem Garawi (7)   82
Dilan Patel (7)   83
Aaliyah McBean (7)   84
Riya Patel (7)   85
Hassan Samawe (8)   86
Luke Tyson (8)   87
Krystella Robinson (8)   88
Hina Rana (8)   89
Laylaa Osman (9)   90
Hanisha Patel (8)   91
Vanessa Smart (8)   92
Ray Phillips (8)   93
Saheethan Sivakumar (9)   94
Alexander Marks (9)   95
Lyric Menya Impraim (8)   96
Prina Patel (9)   97
Suseeven Sarvanantharajah (9)   98
Shuganthan Sarvanantharajah (9)   99
Danny Nguyen (9)   100
Lutfiyya Shaikh (9)   101
Mehreen Qaisrani (11)   102
Luxsiya Sivakumar (11)   103
Prashant Pitroda (10)   104
Eleanor Mark (7)   105
Joseph John-Phillip (8)   106
Waseem Ahmed (7)   107
Mohamed Ali (8)   108
Dishan Tolia (7)   109
Seif Al-Adnani (8)   110
Terrell Telemaque (11)   111
Hanan Mujahid (10)   112

Monique Alexander Fearon (11) 113
Kaiya Nelson (10) 114
Jordan James Moorcroft (10) 115
Yousuf Al-Mousawi (11) 116
Deena Osman (10) 117
Jordan Batchelor (11) 118
Samiyah Bhunnoo (11) 119
Nikita Patel (11) 120
Daijana Joseph (10) 121
Arani Ponnambalathasan (11) 122
Sabrina Saunders (10) 123
Thanusia Veerasingam (11) 124
Zhané Thorpe (11) 125
Ali-Taha Sheikh (11) 126
Saif Khan (11) 127
Kajal Patel (11) 128
Nishit Dhanji (11) 129
Pritam Parmar (10) 130
Aniksha Pindoria (10) 131
Shannon Leigh (10) 132
Nikki Tolia (10) 133

Keep Hatch Primary School, Wokingham
Abigail Raikes (10) 134
Christopher Haggitt (11) 135
Natalie Jackson (11) 136
Jasmin Cheung (11) 137
Jasmine Touchin (11) 138
Oliver Wilson (10) 139
Robert Desson (11) 140
Jamie Macdonald (11) 141
Jenna Smith (11) 142
Megan Lee (11) 143
Zoe Wood (11) 144
Yasmin Castell (11) 145
Elliot Atkinson (11) 146
Felicity Haines (10) 147
Kasey Smith & Paris Nimako (11) 148
Harry Randall & Sami Cengiz (11) 149
Ryan James (10) 150
Kirsty Coleman (11) 151

The Silchester Manor School, Taplow

Winbury School, Maidenhead

The Poems

Esther

I wonder if her life is full,
Or is it maybe really dull?

Does she have a lot of toys?
Does she like a lot of noise?

Is she rich with lots of money,
Or is her food all really runny?

Is there chance to go to ballet,
Or does she live in a straw-mud chalet?

Is she suffering from lack of water?
Are there floods, not getting shorter?

Long ago, lots of murder,
Men that make you shiver and shudder.

Is this all part of her life?

Sophie Osborne (8)
Arborfield Newland & Barkham CE Junior School, Reading

Favourite Things

When I went to South Africa
I swam in the sparkly sea
When I went to South Africa
I caught a shiny fish
When I went to South Africa
I played in the rough sand
When I went to South Africa
I went in a cable car up Table Mountain
When I went to South Africa
My granny made me yummy South African spicy sausages
Called Boerewors
These are the reasons I like it there.

Adam McArthur (7)
Arborfield Newland & Barkham CE Junior School, Reading

Silky

Silky is as lovely as a rose
As fat as a bat
As fast as a cheetah
As dumb as a bun
As soft as cotton
As slow as a slug
As rough as a carpet
As gentle as a lily
As rough as a bully
The best guinea pig in the world
Silky.

Matthew Eames (8)
Arborfield Newland & Barkham CE Junior School, Reading

Seasons

I love to watch the seasons go by

In winter I love to jump in the snow
I wear my snowpants when it is cold

In spring I like it that lots of babies are born
But often, through the rainbow the rain will pour

In summer I love it warm and hot
It feels just like a boiling pot

I love the fact that in summer it is my birthday
I like wearing short things in any kind of way

In autumn I see lots of colours like red, orange, yellow and brown
I like jumping in the piles of leaves that I have found

So this is what I like about our seasons
I can't wait to hear about what you have to say!

Laura Foster (7)
Arborfield Newland & Barkham CE Junior School, Reading

Best Friends

Friends, friends, what are they for?
They are for being there when you are alone
Friends, friends, look out for one another
Friends, friends, have fun together
Friends, friends, are there for one another
Share secrets with one another
Friends, friends, cheer for one another
And laugh a lot together
I am glad I have friends!

Miranda Trevithick (7)
Arborfield Newland & Barkham CE Junior School, Reading

My Pets

I have a fish tank all shiny and new,
I have not one fish, but quite a few.

Pretty colours, red and blue,
Me and my dad watch them too.

They swim happily around,
We watch them together without a sound.

And out in the garden, in our shed,
We have two guinea pigs and their bed.

We feed them every day
With fresh fruit, vegetables and hay.

My sister's is called Snowy,
She is black and white,
Mine is called Liquorice
And is as dark as the night.

Luke Baldwin (8)
Arborfield Newland & Barkham CE Junior School, Reading

My Kitten

I have a fluffy kitten
I love her with all my soul
Her name is Molly Mitten
Her coat's as black as coal.

She has a lovely purr
I like how she is fluffy
She has a lot of fur
And she is very, very scruffy.

She has cute, small paws
Lovely hazel eyes
Very sharp claws and . . .

I bet she would win a prize!

Olivia Whitehouse (9)
Arborfield Newland & Barkham CE Junior School, Reading

My Cat

My cat is called Dale
He's got a long, black, bushy tail
My cat is as huge as a big, blue whale.

One day I saw my cat
He looked so very fat
That I thought he might go *pop!*

He loves his furry bed
More than being fed
It's as soft as a teddy bear.

He tries to catch a mouse
To bring into our house
But Mum is not very happy.

The best bit of all about Dale
Is that he is colourful, cute and cuddly
And I love him lots.

David Reid (7)
Arborfield Newland & Barkham CE Junior School, Reading

The Fat Baby

He is as big as a house
As fat as a ball
He is as cute as a puppy
As strong as a wrestler

As fast as a cheetah
He is as sleepy as a tortoise
As playful as a kitten
That is my baby brother.

Benjamin Dance (8)
Arborfield Newland & Barkham CE Junior School, Reading

What Robert Likes

R obots are the coolest things
O ther things I like have wings
B uzzy bees make me honey
E ven though it costs me money
R obert likes all of these things
T hough I like discovery wings.

Robert Montandon (8)
Arborfield Newland & Barkham CE Junior School, Reading

Ash

He's as cute as a bunny
And snugly too
He cries like a baby
When he is missing you.

He has big owl eyes
To help him see
He's as sneaky as a fox
When he's looking for his tea.

He's as playful as a dolphin
Out at sea
He rolls on his back
For all to see.

He is my little kitten
Who means so much to me
I know he loves me dearly
Because he sleeps next to me.

Calum Galloway (7)
Arborfield Newland & Barkham CE Junior School, Reading

Eros, The Dog Of Love

My dog is
As fast as a cheetah
As smelly as a fish
As warm as a heater.

My dog is
As beautiful as the sunset
As loving as my mum
He is my favourite pet.

My dog's name
Is Eerie
He isn't very scary
He is very cheery.

Louie Hall (8)
Arborfield Newland & Barkham CE Junior School, Reading

The Earth

The Earth is like a bouncing ball
The Earth is like a shopping mall
The Earth is like a spinning top
The Earth is like a swishing mop

The Earth is like a mobile home
The Earth is like a telephone
The Earth is like a great big toy
The Earth is filled with lots of joy.

Holly Chamberlain (8)
Arborfield Newland & Barkham CE Junior School, Reading

It's Big And Hairy

Once, I saw a big and hairy thing,
With gigantic goggle eyes,
He was scruffy and huffy,
Oh, I wish he had been fluffy!

I found him in the sticky, smelly mud,
Digging like a mad dog looking for a bone,
He was scruffy and huffy,
Oh, I wish he had been fluffy!

He followed me to school one day,
It was a big shock for everyone,
He was scruffy and huffy,
Oh, I wish he had been fluffy!

The teachers fainted in fright
The hairy thing ran out of school huffing and puffing,
He was scruffy and huffy,
Oh, I wish he had been fluffy!

The people screamed and hid,
They shouted, 'A hairy thing has gone crazy!'
He was scruffy and huffy,
Oh, I wish he had been fluffy.

But the thing came and shook hands with me,
I thought maybe he was kind,
When people heard the news,
They danced around in glee.

This is where the poem ends!

April Reid (8)
Arborfield Newland & Barkham CE Junior School, Reading

Football

The whistle blows
He kicks the ball
Where it goes
No one knows at all

Down the wing
And into the air
The crowd start to sing
Yippee! It's there!

The back of the net
It hit with force
The goalie with it
Crash! Of course!

Restart the game
And we're 1-0 up
Ten minutes to go
And we win the cup!

Jake McKernan (9)
Arborfield Newland & Barkham CE Junior School, Reading

Friends And Dens!

I have lots of friends
And we all make dens

And in those dens that we make
We eat an enormous cake

And why do we need a cake? I hear you say
Oh, it's to keep us going through the day

In the cake that I make, I put lots of wheat
Although I put in a bit of meat

When a friend says, 'This tastes of meat!'
I just say, 'It's only wheat!'

Cameron Hanson (9)
Arborfield Newland & Barkham CE Junior School, Reading

The Weather

Some days are rainy days
Rainy days are bad
Sunny days are best
Windy days are sort of best
And so are snowy days
On a wet day
You can splash in puddles
On a hot day
You can splash in a paddling pool
On a snowy day
You can have a snowball fight
On a blowy day
You can fly a kite.

Steven Sanderson (8)
Arborfield Newland & Barkham CE Junior School, Reading

Cricket

This is great cricket
What a wicket
Bowlers done a leg bye
Wow! he hit that high!

He bowled a Yorker
What a corker
He's out!
What a shout.

His stumps went flying
Batsman started crying
The bowler was happy
A very happy chappie.

The next batsman came in
Grinning a grin
But with a wonderful catch
The fielders won the match.

Oliver Sankey (8)
Arborfield Newland & Barkham CE Junior School, Reading

My Mum Is An Artist

My mum is good at art,
She's always drawing things.
My mum has a joyful heart,
But I hate it when she sings.

My mum is good at making,
She's great at origami fish.
She always does the baking,
She sometimes breaks the dish.

My mum's name is Suzanne,
But my dad calls her Floss.
She always has a plan,
But it sometimes ends in chaos.

My mum is so kind,
I love my mum so dear.
She's always on my mind,
I'm so glad she's here.

Alabama Hall (8)
Arborfield Newland & Barkham CE Junior School, Reading

The Very Strange Farmer

There once was a very strange farmer,
Who instead of a dog, had a llama.

Cos he couldn't keep up,
With this young boisterous pup
And had found that a llama was calmer.

But the llama was really quite sad,
As the sheep thought him totally mad!

Jessica Prewett (9)
Arborfield Newland & Barkham CE Junior School, Reading

Golden Eagle

G olden feathers like the light
O h, how it blazes in the sun
L ovely white head
D arts through trees
E very time looking for its prey
N o one can catch it.

E yes like bullets
A thunder bolt shooting down
G reat big claws like daggers
L arge beak like a goat's horns
E normous body like an aeroplane.

Ay-Jay Waistell (10)
Cranbourne Primary School, Winkfield

Cobra

He is dangerous
As he squeezes his prey
Till its eyes popped out
He can swallow a goat whole;
Spits venom with a powerful bite
Like a brick dropping on your leg,
Fangs sinking into your arm,
Injecting venom into your body
He bites your veins -
He kills you.

Philip Dunne (10)
Cranbourne Primary School, Winkfield

Witches

Witch's warty, pointy nose
And her ragged old clothes,
Broomsticks flying up high
Into the dark, black sky.

There's a witch striking a spell
And that witch really smells,
Witch's pointy, dirty nails
And she eats slimy snails . . .

There's that witch burying her cat,
There's that witch with her pointy hat,
There's that witch with her new, black, hissing cat
And she's eating a fat, dirty rat.

There's that witch with all her potions,
There's that witch, full of emotions,
There's that witch with a wicked smile,
There's that witch who's really vile.

There's that witch who's really stupid,
There's that witch who killed Cupid,
There's that witch who's really evil,
There's that witch who hates treacle.

Megan Charles (9)
Cranbourne Primary School, Winkfield

Witches

That is the witch,
Her name is Mog,
Stirring her potion,
Now adding a frog.

There's the witch
With her big, black cat,
Flying in the sky
With her long pointed hat.

There goes the witch
On her long, wooden broomstick,
Dashing through the clouds
Like a fast-flowing lunatic.

That's the witch
With her straight black hair,
Frizzy and greasy,
With a spiteful, evil scare.

There's the witch
With a spider on her nose,
Tickling and giggling,
Now crawling on her toes.

There's the witch
Flying in the sky,
Up and up
She's flying so high.

There is the witch
With a long, sharp nose,
Old and broken,
With her itchy, ragged clothes.

Where's the witch?
She's saying goodbye,
Balancing on her broomstick,
Goodbye, goodbye!

Sarah Baker (10)
Cranbourne Primary School, Winkfield

Cheetah

Jumps on its prey,
Runs like a thunderbolt,
Sharp claws, sharp teeth,
Pointy ears, whips with its tail,
Sleeps in trees, chews like a crocodile.
Furry body, skinny, lean and fast,
Teeth like fangs,
Running through the forest,
Killing other animals.
Climbing up trees,
Pouncing on its prey,
Vicious and scary,
Frightens all the animals, chews its prey,
There it goes, running past me,
Like a thunderbolt.

Ryan Harcup (9)
Cranbourne Primary School, Winkfield

Witch

The witches' brooms
Fly through the misty gloom,
Over cliff tops into caves,
Scary witches are so brave.

Diving through the forest and woods,
Covered with their big, black hoods,
In and out of big bushes,
As the wind whooshes.

The witches' chins are long and pointy,
They are singing a happy, little song,
The velvet black cat,
Looks just like a little bat.

The witches' long dresses, tatty and black,
Looking into their big brown sacks,
Warts all bubbly and green,
Such as you have never seen.

Cauldron round and very black,
Shaking their heads, not looking back,
Bubble, bubble,
Looking for trouble!

Sophie Mason (10)
Cranbourne Primary School, Winkfield

Fairies

When fairies are ten
They need a den,
When fairies are nine
They have some wine.

When fairies are eight
They open the gate,
When fairies are seven
They go to Heaven.

When fairies are six
They do tricks,
When fairies are five
They stay alive.

When fairies are four
They kick down the door,
When fairies are three
They fly up a tree.

When fairies are two
They know what to do,
When fairies are one
They are so young.

When a fairy is zero
She'll become a hero.

Sophie Weller (10)
Cranbourne Primary School, Winkfield

Fairies

Fairies fly to distant lands
With their sparkly wings
And little wands in their hands,
They do it in the spring.

They live in Fairyland
With their friends and families,
In the air they do handstands
And they try to hide in trees.

They like fishing for fish,
It smells good from the fire
To my dish,
Always busy, they never retire.

Dancing around the fire is fun,
Fairy children prance all around,
There's lots to do for everyone,
Listen to the cheerful sound.

When children lose their teeth
The fairies will take them away,
Such a quiet little thief,
They might see you today.

With them they bring fairy dust
And sprinkle it above the lands,
A tiny figure you can trust,
With magic little hands.

Saffron Hothi (9)
Cranbourne Primary School, Winkfield

Dragons

Quickly flying over white mountains,
Slurping slowly from water fountains,
Lurking in cold, dark corners,
Their great big eyes glisten through the dark,
Spying on a drinking lark.

The dragon's hot breath is burning,
Sharply are the corners turning,
Their ripping, sharp, dagger-like claws,
Their mossy green scales,
Pointy sharp spikes down their tails.

Their scaly, leathery wings,
Their bites that sting,
The dragon's roar is drowning,
The creamy breast, goes up and down,
Scorching innocent towns.

Their home is in a forest or two,
Eating cows that go moo,
Their claws are ripping,
Destroying palaces,
Going to any place.

Hiding in dark corners,
Waiting to bite,
With a big crunch,
Their wings trying,
Flapping and flying.

Between his teeth, meat is stuck
And the dragon needs luck
To get it out,
Scorching towns
And swooping quickly down.

Kira Eley (10)
Cranbourne Primary School, Winkfield

Cheetah

Pounces on its prey
Sleeps in the day
Runs like lightning
Is very frightening
And never leaves its prey.

He hides like a crocodile
And sometimes runs a mile
He lives in secret dens
And eats a hen
While he is in his den.

Oliver Betteridge (10)
Cranbourne Primary School, Winkfield

Fairies

The little fairies spread their wings
And fly above the trees,
The tiny fairies get on the birds
And fly across the seas.

The good-natured, magical creatures
With wings like dragonflies,
Dressed in colourful petals
They meet up with butterflies.

The acorn cups for bowls
And carved twigs for spoons,
The fairies skip around flowers
On all the afternoons.

With tiny hands and dainty feet
They tiptoe across the ground,
With little smiles upon their faces
They flutter all around.

The cooking fairies bake
The food and they're called brownies,
The dancing fairies sing along
And they are called pixies.

The fairies fly across the land
And watch over you and me,
The boggarts run across the ground
And annoy us, 'Tee-hee-hee!'

It's time to say goodbye, farewell,
I hope to see you soon,
Maybe you could see the fairies
On a summer's afternoon.

Rosemary Gosztonyi (10)
Cranbourne Primary School, Winkfield

Dragons

The big green dragon
Smashed the brown wagon,
His massive, daggery claws
Break all the laws,
Roaring as loud as a train.

His spiky black teeth, crunching
And also munching,
The spooky big blue eyes
And the wings that make him fly
As high as a plane.

The hot fiery breath,
Burning people to death,
Ping . . . pong . . .
The dragon's gone!
Never to be seen again.

Danielle Malyon (10)
Cranbourne Primary School, Winkfield

A Fairy Tale

Floating, falling,
Someone's calling,
Who can it be?
Who can I see?
Someone's staring at me,
That's all I can see -
Slinky wings
And cobwebby things;
Now I can see a little light
And it is so bright.

Something fluttered about,
Shocked, I gave a shout,
There was no one to be seen,
Who could it have been?
Who was that?
I saw a hat . . .
I looked down with a shrug
And saw a hole someone had dug . . .

I fell in,
I couldn't breathe,
I grabbed something
And climbed back up
And ran away so quickly!

Emma Weller (10)
Cranbourne Primary School, Winkfield

Fairies

Fairies fly,
High in the sky,
They spread out their wings
And start to sing.

I can't understand why,
They fly so high,
They love to sing
And signal with their wings.

In the sky they swirl
And on the ground, they twirl,
Leaving a trail of fairy dust,
Really is a must.

Echo Marriott (9)
Cranbourne Primary School, Winkfield

Dragon Flames

I saw a dragon
Who crushed a wagon,
His eyes were burning red,
Before I knew it
He'd crushed someone's head.
I was scared to death,
He had such burning breath,
I tried to run,
Without a hope,
Despite my precious gun.
He had giant wings
And spiky things
Down to his knee,
I wish I was at home,
Watching my TV.
He had deadly claws
And powerful jaws,
Then he smashed down
All the houses
And ate all the mouses!

Jason Mangru (9)
Cranbourne Primary School, Winkfield

The Tooth Fairy

This is a poem about a fairy
Who is very small,
She has tiny wings
And she wishes to be tall.

She has golden, twinkly hair
And is dressed in white,
With a glistening wand
And she has pink, clear skin.

She swoops across the land
And across the clear blue sea,
As high as the birds
And to see you and me.

She sneaks into houses
And children's bedrooms,
To find a tooth
And replaces it with money.

She visits all her friends,
Elves, pixies and flower fairies,
She is very popular
With everyone.

Kind, gentle and funny,
Is what she is,
All her friends and family
Adore her very much.

Kate Deans (10)
Cranbourne Primary School, Winkfield

Witches

Their ragged clothes
And pointy noses,
The broomstick with the cat
That sits on the back
And goes *hiss* and *spit*.

The cauldron with
The green bubbles,
Witches cause
Double trouble.

Witches put
Frogs and rats
And yellow toenails
Into the cauldron.

This poison will
Turn children
Into mice
Never to return to human.

This poison may cost a child his life.

Olivia Vine (10)
Cranbourne Primary School, Winkfield

The Royal Banquet

Golden platters laid on a huge, oak table,
Silver cutlery shining in the light,
Royal people sit on velvet-cushioned thrones,
While servants serve the salad starter.

Cold chicken in a leafy salad
Topped with a tangy Caesar sauce,
Hilarious jesters amuse the laughing audience,
When everyone is ready, here comes the second course.

Spare meaty-ribs full of flavour
With a bowl of barbeque sauce,
When all the meat is gone
The third course is ready.

Sausages wrapped with crispy bacon,
Jacket potatoes full of cheese,
Chicken in a meaty gravy,
Carrots and peas and green broccoli.

Everyone's been waiting for the pudding,
Always people's favourite course,
Servants cooking it for two hours,
They've been doing kitchen chores.

A rich, brown, huge chocolate fountain,
With fruit to dip in the sauce,
People crowding around the vast colossus,
They all want more and more and more.

Chocolate pudding with ripe, round cherries,
Served with a jug of thick, white cream,
Servants carry the plates away,
Preparing for tomorrow's feast.

Archie Luckhurst (9)
Cranbourne Primary School, Winkfield

Witch

Witch of the west,
Her broomstick beats the rest,
From her black, pointy hat,
To her fat, tubby cat.

Her poisonous potions,
Can change a man to beast,
With a wave of her hand,
They disappear to an unknown land.

Her cooking is nasty
And very ghastly,
She eats dragon's liver,
It might make you shiver.

She cooks her food in a cauldron
Over a burning fire
And eats her woodlice
Near the heat and warmth.

Amy Balmforth (9)
Cranbourne Primary School, Winkfield

Dragons

Big mouth, sharp teeth, big tail,
Gigantic;
Pointy scales, big feet, long wings,
Humungous;
Disgusting breath, fierce fire,
Enormous;
Dragon's gobble you up in one,
Yum, yum, yum!

Screeching, screaming,
Scary;
Yelling, bellowing,
Roaring;
Screeching, squealing,
Shrieking;
Dragon's gobble you up in one,
Yum, yum, yum!

Scratching, grazing,
Scraping;
Marking, blemishing,
Claws out;
Living, dying, drowning, surviving,
Sinking;
Dragon's gobble you up in one,
Yum, yum, yum!

Fighting, biting, clashing,
Disputing;
Opposing, quarrelling,
Scrambling;
Hard, firm, stiff,
Tough;
Dragon's are very bad,
Bad, bad, bad, bad!

Adelle Caines (9)
Cranbourne Primary School, Winkfield

If I Had Wings

(Based on 'If I Had Wings' by Pie Corbett)

If I had wings,
I would feel the pointy stars.

If I had wings,
I would eat the candyfloss clouds.

If I had wings,
I would hear the planets whisper to each other.

If I had wings,
I would smell the sweet raindrops.

If I had wings,
I would see the jewelled moon.

If I had wings,
I'd hover across the vast ocean.

If I had wings,
That's what I'd dream of.

William Smith (9)
Downsway Primary School, Reading

Fears!

I'm afraid of graveyards at night,
Even a spider's bite.

I'm terrified of bears,
They give me frights and scares.

Frankenstein's monster makes me jump,
In the night I hear a *bump!*

I'm scared stiff
Of falling off a cliff.

In the night I hear a *bang!*
It might be a ghost gang.

I hide under my bed,
Afraid that over there is something dead.

Reece Weatherley (9)
Downsway Primary School, Reading

A Meal Of Words

Last night at dinner,
I tasted a bit,
I nibbled and pecked,
Then I dined, swallowed
And chewed and gobbled,
The food was so good
I even devoured my plate!

Alex Winn (9)
Downsway Primary School, Reading

A River's Story

Rumbling rapids racing by,
For canoeists to compete and have fun.
Puppy dogs paddling,
Pleasantly slurping up my fresh, new water,
Boat parties,
Loudly beating past,
Fish diving,
Dodging through weeds and past stones,
Fishermen fishing,
For the heaviest fish,
Swans, swiftly swimming,
On my water,
Everyone likes me,
I'm the river!

Bethan Thomas (10)
Downsway Primary School, Reading

A Trip To White Hart Lane

My heart was beating furiously,
Davids' shot hit the crossbar,
Super shot!
End of the first half.

Let's get some delicious hot dogs!
Before you know,
It's the second half
And it's a goal!

The fans go wild,
Defoe scores,
I finish my drink and my hot dog,
Wait a minute!
Defoe scores again!

My team has thrashed Porto!
I am so excited!
Home now, happy and tired.

Oliver Smith (9)
Downsway Primary School, Reading

A Meal Of Words

I was so hungry last night that
I gobbled grapes,
Swallowed cereal,
Bit a biscuit
And nibbled noodles.
I dined on doughnuts
And chewed on chips,
Until at last, I was full!

Toby Herman (9)
Downsway Primary School, Reading

Green Is . . .

Green is grass,
Swaying in the meadow.
Green is an apple,
As crunchy as can be.

Green is jealousy,
Greed and sickness.
Green is somebody
As thick as thickness.

Green is the meadow
And mid-summer leaves.
Green is the stain
When you fall on your knees.

Amy Hatter (9)
Downsway Primary School, Reading

When I Won My First Ever Football Match

Not long now to kick-off,
All the anxious players raring to go,
Ready for the second half.
The ref blew the whistle,
I ran in for the ball,
I got it running down the wing,
All on my own in front of the goal,
I could hear my manager shouting, 'Shoot!'
I took my position and in the count of three,
I smacked the ball as hard as I could.
'Goal!' I shouted as it hit the crossbar and bounced in,
Then the ref blew his whistle for full-time,
At last, we had won the exhausting match!

Jack Mintern (9)
Downsway Primary School, Reading

Green Is . . .

Green is grass,
Swaying in the breeze.
Green is leaves,
Waving on the trees.

Green is the colour
Of the middle of your eye.
Green is the apple
In the middle of a crumbly pie.

Green is a frog,
Leap, boing, bounce!
Green is a lizard
Ready to pounce.

Green is broccoli,
Brussels sprouts and peas
And green is a stalk,
If you please.

Maisie Pitchford (10)
Downsway Primary School, Reading

Green Is . . .

Green is a frog that jumps in the air,
Green is a grasshopper who gives you a scare,
Green is sickness when you're not well,
Green is peppers that you try to sell.

Traffic lights are green to tell you to go,
Peas, lettuce, runner beans, *no, no, no!*
The colour green can make you sad
And make you feel so gloomy and mad.

Sarah Lawrence (10)
Downsway Primary School, Reading

What's He Like?

He's a rock,
But can be a bull in a china shop.
He's a chip off the old block,
He's worth his weight in gold,
The salt of the Earth.
But when he's under the weather,
He's a bit of a donkey,
He sleeps like a log,
He is a star
He can be a bossy boots,
But he is a good friend to me.

Daniel Holmes (10)
Downsway Primary School, Reading

Fears!

I'm frightened of a rat,
Creeping round the house
And scared of a snake,
Trying to eat a mouse,
I hate creepy-crawlies,
Tiptoeing round my room
And terrified of monsters,
Making a big boom,
I'm afraid of ghosts,
Swooping far and near
And scared stiff of spiders,
So that's my biggest fear.

Tabitha Grove (9)
Downsway Primary School, Reading

Well Said!

When my mum told me off
I screamed, I argued, I shouted, I cried,
I ranted and raged, I pleaded and sighed,
I moaned and groaned,
I begged and I swore,
But all my mum did
Was just slam the door!

Jamie Gorman (10)
Downsway Primary School, Reading

Green Is . . .

Green is a snake
Or moss on a rake,
A fresh new leaf
Falling down to the ground.

Green is jealousy,
Envy or greed,
It can even be
A mouldy seed.

Green can be slimy
And also grimy
And green is just
So very limey.

Connor Froude (10)
Downsway Primary School, Reading

Our New Neighbours

Our new neighbours are crazy
And even sometimes lazy.

They never wash their car,
Instead they go to the bar.

They have a lot to drink,
When they come home, they stink!

In their garden they have a pond,
Of which I am very fond.

A frog sits on the side,
I'm sure that it has died!

It's been there for so long,
I've just named him King Pong!

Their garden is over-grown,
I always hear them moan.

They shout out in the street,
Which makes me stamp my feet.

They are moving very soon,
Hopefully, to the moon!

Louella Minter (10)
Downsway Primary School, Reading

A River's Story

Watch out!
I'm going to overflow!
I'll flood your street,
Your town
And even your house,
Better move quickly, before it's too late!

I'll shove your car if you don't move,
Quickly, before I overflow.
I'll stop you from getting in and out of your house,
Hurry, before it's too late!

I wreck buildings,
I will destroy your homes,
I'll make you cry your eyes out,
Hurry, before it's too late!

Luke Gracey (9)
Downsway Primary School, Reading

Fears!

Frightening animals wander and roam,
Rhinos are fierce and powerful,
Iguanas slither secretly like baby dragons
And gorillas, hairy and scary, really petrify me!

Horses galloping fast and furious,
Tarantulas with their dangerous bite,
Elephants that stomp and stamp,
Noisy chickens that pierce my ear
And deadly scorpions jab their prey.

Andrew Childs (9)
Downsway Primary School, Reading

School Holidays

Ah! This is the life,
The tide strolling in,
What could be better,
Than having a month off school!

Ah! First in France,
With its master chefs.
America could be next,
After all, it's the future.
Spain sounds promising,
Sandy, sunny, sumptuous beaches.
Greece is a dream
Of some of Olympia's architects.
Australia's outback,
A place of wildlife.

I'll be back to school,
Soon enough!

Cameron Murgatroyd (9)
Downsway Primary School, Reading

If I Had Wings

(Based on 'If I Had Wings' by Pie Corbett)

If I had wings,
I could run my fingers against the clouds
And feel the dampness.

If I had wings,
I would taste them
And savour the raindrops in my mouth.

If I had wings,
I could hear the sweet birds
Tweet their heavenly tune.

If I had wings,
I would breathe in all the fresh air I could.

If I had wings,
I would gaze down at all the tiny figures below.

If I had wings,
I would dream about every next day's wonders.

Connor Almond (9)
Downsway Primary School, Reading

A River's Story

Up in the hills I start,
I can't wait to go down,
What's below?
I'm a sparkling spring, flowing down.
I see hungry birds swooping around, looking for their dinner.
Now I'm a glittering stream,
As I tumble over the rocks,
I'm as clear as glass.
Now it's summer,
I'm dried up,
A tiny trickle
On cracked mud.
I can't wait
Till the rains of
Autumn make
Me bigger.
Now I'm a strong, raging river,
But I'm muddy and cold,
With rubbish, bottles float on my surface.
It's springtime and people on boats
Put the tips of their fingers into me
And play with my water.
I'm getting wider now and deeper and slower and slower.
I'm near the mouth and now I'm out,

Out into

The open

Sea.

Lewis Davies (10)
Downsway Primary School, Reading

If I Had Wings

(Based on 'If I Had Wings' by Pie Corbett)

If I had wings, I would soar above the clouds
And feel the heat rise by drawing nearer to the sun.

I want to fly high,
Where no one can reach me.

If I had wings, I would savour the sun,
As hot as a bottle of Five Skull chilli sauce.

I want to fly high,
Where no one can reach me.

If I had wings, I would listen to the traffic jams
And rush-hours down below.

I want to fly high,
Where no one can reach me.

If I had wings, I would smell all the cities
And towns below me.

I want to fly high,
Where no one can reach me.

If I had wings, I would fly an inch above the sea
And gaze at my reflection in the water,
As my wings shimmer in the summer sun.

I want to fly high,
Where no one can reach me.

If I had wings, I would realise it was only a dream.

I want to fly high,
Where no one can reach.

Ryan Davey (10)
Downsway Primary School, Reading

A Meal Of Words

When the lion caught the antelope,
He devoured and he gobbled,
He swallowed and chomped,
He scoffed and he chewed
And dined on his food.
He bit at the meat,
Then nibbled the tail
And ate the last morsel,
Then he was full.

Andrew Allen (9)
Downsway Primary School, Reading

Peacock

Peacock
Bright colours
Blue, yellow, orange
Feathers eyes everywhere
Silent, cal, beautiful, colourful birds
White beak, blue neck and head
How and why are peacocks so colourful?

Max Keel (9)
East Court School for Dyslexia, Ramsgate

Hallowe'en Night

N ew moon comes out
I magine trees blowing in the wind
G oing back onto the motorway
H ome to find a ghost
T onight *all* the ghosts come out.

William Catchpole
East Court School for Dyslexia, Ramsgate

Night-Time

N ervous of the dark, no one in the house
I n and out of sleep
G hosts in the cupboard
H owling and screaming, hooting and pounding
T ime to wake up, go to school with no sleep.

Jonathon Spurin (11)
East Court School for Dyslexia, Ramsgate

The Kitten

Kitten
Fluffy, pink
Cute and listening
Quiet as a mouse
Ginger as gingerbread
At last, it found its mother.

Oliver Hadman (10)
East Court School for Dyslexia, Ramsgate

The Tiger

Strong
Cute, fluffy
Staring, angry, calm
Orange, white, black, blue
The tiger pounces through water
Why, I ask, are tigers so mysterious?

William Colyer (9)
East Court School for Dyslexia, Ramsgate

Bears In The Snow

White
Polar bears
Black, tiny eyes
Playing in the snow
Frosty, crunchy, soft, cold snow
Calm bears, sharp claws, furry coats.

Sam Draper (11)
East Court School for Dyslexia, Ramsgate

Night - Haiku

It's a spooky night
You get a terrible fright
Without knowing why.

Petrok Lawrence (10)
East Court School for Dyslexia, Ramsgate

Night - Haiku

Night, dark, scary moon
In the scariest castle
Looking at the bats.

Peter Caspell (10)
East Court School for Dyslexia, Ramsgate

Night

N obody is in the house
I cy winds blowing at night
G listening and shining moon keeping me awake
H iding under my cover
T ense at night.

Matthew Pelizzoli (10)
East Court School for Dyslexia, Ramsgate

Night

Night is as black as coal
Like a gaping black hole
The silvery moon and stars
And the faint hum of cars
A glow of orange light from a lamp post
And the grey mist of a ghost
In the morning there will be light
And there will be no more night.

Maddie Ford (10)
East Court School for Dyslexia, Ramsgate

Zebras

Bold
Cold eyes
Pushing and shoving
Thin, long legs marching
Stripes in black and white
Yellow sunset on the horizon
The zebras march to a better place.

Eve Ricketts (11)
East Court School for Dyslexia, Ramsgate

Koala

Koala
Sitting there
In the tree
Nothing can disturb him
Munching away at the leaves
Dreaming
Far away
Sunlight gleaming through
No sound at all.

Callum McGregor (10)
East Court School for Dyslexia, Ramsgate

Easter Egg

Egg
Juicy egg
Chocolate, juicy egg
Spotty egg, round egg
Colourful, white, stripy egg
Red, blue, green egg.

Charles Connell (9)
East Court School for Dyslexia, Ramsgate

The City

City
Big city
Hot, sunny city
A large, colourful city
Lots of people in the city
A big, grey wall
A big, strong wall protecting the city.

Max Ellison (10)
East Court School for Dyslexia, Ramsgate

Night

The starry night
The camp fire light
Seeing Orion's belt glisten in the dark night
Seeing our universe float by
What a mystery to us all
Everything so quiet
Except for the rustling of the trees
And the waves hitting the rocks
Small pinpricks of light in the distance
Night is over!

Sean Gilligan (11)
East Court School for Dyslexia, Ramsgate

Night

Night looks like a huge black sheet,
Covering the city,
In the city the lights shine brightly,
Never going off,
Cars and buses driving past.

In the countryside, the stars glisten in the night sky,
Animals scurrying around looking for shelter,
The tall trees rustle together.

For the little children, night is dark and scary,
Monsters and ghouls come out to play,
Staying up all night, until the sun comes out.

For me, the night is good,
I like listening to the rain on my window,
I enjoy listening to the wind blowing things about in the garden
And then slowly drifting off to sleep.

Luke Lennard (10)
East Court School for Dyslexia, Ramsgate

The Vikings Who Fought Our School

The day the Vikings came to call,
They sliced the school's best, big, cool ball
And made Reception's Lego fall,
After smashing Nursery's play set mall,
Then they destroyed the school's big hall.

They fought in the infant playground,
Then they killed the head teacher's hound,
After they made a dreadful sound,
They broke the board with one big pound,
Then they lost their shields which were round.

Sulakshan Ranaweera (8)
Elsley Primary School, Wembley

The Romans Fought Our School

The day the Romans came to our school,
They thought they were very, very cool,
They were hot, so they went into the pool,
Then they acted like really dumb fools,
After they saw some beautiful jewels.

The Romans did not know what to say,
So they covered the head with some hay,
They had to do lots of things, like pay,
After the head thought of the beautiful day
And then they shouted, 'Yay!'

Sahra Jama (8)
Elsley Primary School, Wembley

The Vikings Raid The School

The day the Vikings came to raid on their ships,
Wracked the school to shreds and on their hips,
There were swords so sharp like a knife, their lips
Looks like lipstick, they were eating chips,
Like crazy and the bad Viking killed a person called Tips.

The Vikings came to land
On the English sand,
They chopped off people's hands
And left them on a stand,
They were such an evil band.

Mohammed Ayyub Khan (8)
Elsley Primary School, Wembley

The Day The Vikings Came To Steal

The day the Vikings came to steal,
They broke all the window seals,
But then they wanted a meal,
So then they came to steal a peel,
The children wondered how their master would feel.

This time was the Vikings' end,
We had lots of stuff to mend,
But they had always done a bend,
So the children had a letter to send
And the master had to lend.

The day the Vikings said to us, 'Shoo!'
They had a cow that said, 'Moo, moo!'
We tried to scare them with, 'Boo!'
Some of them were in twos
And one of them had some poo!

Noor Salem Garawi (7)
Elsley Primary School, Wembley

The Day The Vikings Invaded School

The Vikings made the teacher a fool
And the children thought it was cool,
Then they threw the paint in the pool,
So they threw water on the school,
Then the Vikings broke the school's rule.

The Vikings broke some things,
Then came the powerful kings,
Then the Vikings found some wings,
The Celts brought some rings,
Then the Vikings stones did bring.

Dilan Patel (7)
Elsley Primary School, Wembley

The Vikings Who Came To Invade

One day the Vikings came in their long ships
Carrying swords on their hips
The ladies had red lips
Then they saw nits.
The monks said, 'Good, now turn into bits!'
The monks are cool,
'We can beat you up like a mule!'
'No you can't, you'll need to be cruel!'
'Just shut up you fools!'
'You can't swim in pools!'

Aaliyah McBean (7)
Elsley Primary School, Wembley

The Vikings Who Invaded

The Vikings have lots of things,
The Vikings cannot sing,
The Vikings don't bring stuff,
The Vikings have lots of rings,
The Vikings looked like kings.

The day the Vikings came to fight,
The shields and swords looked really bright
And the tough ones looked like knights,
The Vikings went like knights
They didn't see, because of the light.

Riya Patel (7)
Elsley Primary School, Wembley

Britain And Rome

One day the Romans came to Britain from Rome
They tried to burn down all the homes
But they got hit with a bone
Rome got blinded with some foam
Then the Romans started to moan.

Then Britain said, 'Shut up, Rome!'
Rome swore back in an angry tone
They burned down the Emperor's home!
The leader got a stone
And threw it at the commander of Rome!

Hassan Samawe (8)
Elsley Primary School, Wembley

The Day The Vikings Came To School

The Vikings came to school,
They were very, very cool,
They overloaded the pool,
They acted like a fool,
So they got a big tool.

They made the children sad,
Then they killed their angry dad,
Then the Vikings became sad
Then they became good lads.

Luke Tyson (8)
Elsley Primary School, Wembley

Poetry

P oems are fun

O ther poems are boring

E very day in poems you can write about the world

M any people write what they want

S ometimes it rhymes.

Krystella Robinson (8)
Elsley Primary School, Wembley

The Sea

The sea is bright and blue
And splashes on the shore,
The silent sea gushes all around,
The shells spread in the sea and make a whooshing sound.

The sea can be rough and the sea can be calm,
Loud as a seagull and sometimes as silent as a crab,
Swishing from side to side and all around.

Hina Rana (8)
Elsley Primary School, Wembley

The Tropical Trees

The tropical trees sway in the wild rainforest,
By the waterfall flowing gently,
The tropical trees swing gracefully as the wind blows a force
To knock off the coconuts
The colourful birds spread their wings and fly.

The tropical trees sway in the wild rainforest,
Looks at the exotic plants,
The tropical trees and the fine leaves,
All the animals have lots of fun,
The rainforest is a wonderful place to be.

Can you see the tropical trees?

Laylaa Osman (9)
Elsley Primary School, Wembley

Easter Bunny!

It's a lovely spring day
And eggs are hatching,
New blossoms come out,
Birds are flying in fresh air,
New life has been born,
Bluebells swishing side to side,
Trees are growing,
But now babies cry,
Easter eggs are cracking,
Chocolate ripples in your mouth,
Easter is here!

Hanisha Patel (8)
Elsley Primary School, Wembley

Swirly Whirly

A curly line going round and round
To hypnotise you
It is like two different kinds of colours
Going round and round
Like in Mona the Vampire
At the beginning when they start the film.

Vanessa Smart (8)
Elsley Primary School, Wembley

Groovy Guitar

I like electric guitars
They are cool
Rock stars play theirs
Like they are on Mars.
They are cool
Like an iPod
Many people try to get them
But they're all expensive
Electric guitars are cool
Because they are so cruel
I also like guitars
Because they are big like a pig
And tall like they are going to fall.

Ray Phillips (8)
Elsley Primary School, Wembley

The Snowflakes

The snow is like
A soft ice cream
Falling from the sky.
If you touch it
For a year
You will turn white.
Sometimes people
Get a cold
If they play in the snow.
People think snow only comes
On Christmas Day
But snow can come any day, anytime.
People get presents on Christmas Day
Snowflakes come with the snow.

Saheethan Sivakumar (9)
Elsley Primary School, Wembley

The Best Poem Ever!

P oems are fun to read in a book
O ther poems are so funny
E xcellent poems are so good
M y school's poems are good
S ome poems are like magic.

Alexander Marks (9)
Elsley Primary School, Wembley

Poetry

P oems make me dance
O ur magic poems
E ach poem is lovely
M agic poems
S ometimes poems make me laugh.

Lyric Menya Impraim (8)
Elsley Primary School, Wembley

Poems In School

P oems in schools are fun
O cean poems are fun to read
E ating when you are writing a poem is fun
M ore poems to read is fantastic
S chool poems are great!

Prina Patel (9)
Elsley Primary School, Wembley

Sunny Summer

In the summer the sun is out,
If you're lucky you can eat a cream bun,
Sunflower seeds are planted in summer,
After a little while, they grow up to be sunflowers.

In the sea the water is hot,
Put the seeds in a flowerpot,
Icy ice creams are eaten,
The sun is shining in the sky.

Build sandcastles on the seashore,
Buy buckets and spades to make them,
You can feel very happy on the beach,
The beach is very relaxing.

Suseeven Sarvanantharajah (9)
Elsley Primary School, Wembley

The Seasons

In winter the snow falls,
Building snowmen,
Playing snowball fights,
It's fun, fun, fun,
People play on sledges.

In spring the blossom grows,
Rabbits and animals come out,
Flowers grow,
Leaves come out on trees,
Grass grows.

In autumn the leaves fall off trees,
Turn different colours,
Red, orange, yellow, green,
The wind blows the leaves,
Falling down to the ground.

In summer the sun shines,
It's hot, hot, hot,
People go to the beach,
People drink cool water,
Seasons are wonderful!

Shuganthan Sarvanantharajah (9)
Elsley Primary School, Wembley

Football

F ootball is a sport that is played with a ball
O lden days people played football
O ften countries play tournaments to win cups
T housands of people play football
B alls are used in football matches
A ll countries play football
L ots of people like football
L oads and loads of tournaments are played by people.

Danny Nguyen (9)
Elsley Primary School, Wembley

Super Seasons

Seasons are fantastic, seasons are fun,
It's so boring when there is none.

Snow is the best of all,
Go outside, don't stay in the mall.

Autumn is the worst,
No one ever thinks it'll be the first.

Sunny the sun gives everyone a fun time,
Especially when you have a drink of lime.

Super spring is the *most* beautiful of all,
It'll be the most beautiful if you go to the waterfall.

Lutfiyya Shaikh (9)
Elsley Primary School, Wembley

Excited

Excited is the colour baby blue
Excited feels like smooth feathers
Excited looks like rainbow flowers
Excited tastes like ice cream
Excited smells like wild roses
Excited sounds like newborn babies crying
I felt really excited when my mum had a baby.

Mehreen Qaisrani (11)
Elsley Primary School, Wembley

Excitement

Excitement is as colourful as the rainbow
Excitement is like walking on popping popcorn
Excitement tastes of sherbet on the tip of my tongue
Excitement smells of pizza right on my plate
Excitement sounds like people laughing all around me
Excitement looks like a shooting star in the night sky
I get excited when I am on holiday.

Luxsiya Sivakumar (11)
Elsley Primary School, Wembley

Surprise

Surprise is the colour of a rainbow
It feels like a dream come true
It tastes like a box of chocolates
It smells like a French bottle of perfume
It looks like a world of chocolate
It sounds like a singing bird
I get surprised when I get very good presents.

Prashant Pitroda (10)
Elsley Primary School, Wembley

The Day The Vikings Invaded Our School

The day the Vikings came to call,
They burnt the gate, the entrance hall
And popped and kicked a big football,
So they broke the wall and called to all
So tall they were and had to fall.

The Vikings brought their shiny knight
And their weapons were very bright,
So they fought in the night
And then they saw a big light,
They couldn't fight, 'cause they saw a kite.

Eleanor Mark (7)
Elsley Primary School, Wembley

The Vikings Who Invaded Our School

The Vikings from the past came to our school
And everyone was acting like a fool,
They destroyed the staffroom, gym and playground wall
And the nice, clean swimming pool.

The school was going mad,
Someone thought the Vikings weren't bad,
They were making the children frightened and sad.

Shields smashed windows which were bright,
The leader came along with a fright,
He didn't know the Vikings had such might,
But then the Vikings were out of sight,
They leaped into the air with spite.

It's thanks to them we've been freed,
We needn't write, we needn't read,
Me and my mates all agreed,
We didn't go to school for Christmas, Easter or Eid,
So clear the way, let them proceed.

Two years later we came back to school,
We stared at the broken hall
And Reception's play set mall,
Our gang leader said, 'The Vikings were so cool!'

Joseph John-Phillip (8)
Elsley Primary School, Wembley

The Vikings Who Burned Our School

They burned the class
And the glass
And they opened the class door
And went back outside
And got some grass
And they killed a lass.

The Vikings fought the Romans
And one of the Vikings bit someone's hand
So they couldn't fight
They thought they might come to fight
And they went to fight at night
They went forward, then right
And there were no lights
And the people were all right.

Waseem Ahmed (7)
Elsley Primary School, Wembley

Egil The Viking's Strange Shield

Egil the Viking has a strange shield
It's got wheels and springs and seven colours
And this is what they do.

Touch colour number one
It will give you a gun
Touch colour number two
It will make you blue
Touch colour number three
It will make you climb a tree
Touch colour number four
It will open a door
Touch colour number five
It will dip and dive
Touch colour number six
It will make you eat Weetabix
Touch colour number seven
It will make you fly up to Heaven.

Egil the Viking has a strange shield
It's got wheels and springs and seven colours.

Mohamed Ali (8)
Elsley Primary School, Wembley

Egil The Viking's Strange Boat

It will make you say, 'Moo!'
It's got ten rowers and nine strings
And this is what they do.

Pull string number one
It will shoot like a gun
Pull string number two
It will clean your shoe
Pull string number three
It will start to say, *'Weeeee!'*
Pull string number four
It will break my door
Pull string number five
The Viking will start to drive
Pull string number six
The water will start to mix
Pull string number seven
It will go to Devon
Pull string number eight
It will give you a mate
Pull string number nine
The Viking will be kind.

Egil the Viking has a strange boat
It will make you say, 'Moo!'
It's got ten rowers and nine strings
And I wish I had one too!

Dishan Tolia (7)
Elsley Primary School, Wembley

Egil The Viking's Strange Shield

Egil the Viking has a strange shield
It will make you jump when it says, 'Boo!'
It's got switches, batteries and buttons
And this is what they do.

Press button number one
It will make you shoot a gun
Press button number two
It will make you say, 'Ooh!'
Press button number three
It will make you climb a tree
Press button number four
It will make you turn into a door
Press button number five
It will make you stay alive
Press button number six
It will make you eat Weetabix
Press button number seven
It will turn your name into Kevin.

Egil the Viking has a strange shield
It will make you jump when it says, 'Boo!'
It's got switches, batteries and buttons
And I wish I had one too!

Seif Al-Adnani (8)
Elsley Primary School, Wembley

Happy

Happy is the colour pink
It feels like all your dreams are coming true
It looks like the best rose
It tastes like strawberry ice cream
It smells like fried chips
It sounds like 50 Cent songs
I was happy when I got my mini motorbike.

Terrell Telemaque (11)
Elsley Primary School, Wembley

Sad

Sad is the colour black of a basement
It feels like a rough rock at the bottom of the sea
It looks like a broken cottage that was made out of sticks
It tastes like a dead leaf in a dark, creepy forest
It sounds like a zebra being attacked by a predator
I felt sad when I was coming back from Pakistan to England.

Hanan Mujahid (10)
Elsley Primary School, Wembley

Excited

Excited is the colours orange and yellow
Excited feels like you're going on a really fast roller coaster
Excited tastes like sweet, sweet sweets
Excited smells like fresh flowers
Excited sounds like people laughing
Excited looks like the ocean moving.

I was excited when I was going to the fair
I was excited when I did a dare
I was excited when I saw a bear
And I was excited when my mum cared.

Monique Alexander Fearon (11)
Elsley Primary School, Wembley

Shy

Shy is the colour purple
It feels like hiding under your soft covers
It smells like strawberries
It tastes like mashed potatoes
It looks like a girl shaking
It sounds like a bell
I got shy when I was dancing in the X-Factor.

Kaiya Nelson (10)
Elsley Primary School, Wembley

Sad

Sad is the colour white
It feels like the feather of a dove rubbing against your hand
It tastes like ice cream and not tasting a flavour
It smells like a rose growing in summer
It looks like a wet rainy day
It sounds like a slow song
I felt sad when my nan died.

Jordan James Moorcroft (10)
Elsley Primary School, Wembley

Boredom

Boredom is the colour grey
Boredom feels like an endless, still time
It tastes like tasteless chewing gum
It smells like a wonderful scent slowly edging away
Boredom looks like a plain mist
It sounds like a deserted world
I get bored when there is nothing to do.

Yousuf Al-Mousawi (11)
Elsley Primary School, Wembley

Shy

Shy is the colour baby pink
Shy feels like a group of 100 butterflies in my stomach
Shy looks like forgetting my lines in a concert
Shy tastes like a sour lemon
Shy smells like a bunch of violets
Shy sounds like birds whistling and flapping their wings
I was very shy when I was on the X-Factor!

Deena Osman (10)
Elsley Primary School, Wembley

Emotions

I feel angry when people bully and fight
I feel angry when people don't do right.

I feel sad when people die,
I feel sad when people cry.

I feel embarrassed when my sister pulls down my pants,
I feel embarrassed when I'm afraid of ants.

I feel tired when I start to run,
I feel tired when there's no more fun.

I will be happy when there's peace,
In the north, west, south and east.

Jordan Batchelor (11)
Elsley Primary School, Wembley

Excited

Excited is the colour bright blue
It feels like soft clouds and candyfloss
It smells like flowers in a pretty garden
It tastes like bubblegum
It looks like birds flying over the ocean
It sounds like stars twinkling at night and the moon shining
I get excited when I go swimming
With thousands of pupils having a big race.

Samiyah Bhunnoo (11)
Elsley Primary School, Wembley

Anger

The colour of anger is red
It feels like an erupting volcano exploding in your head
It looks like a dull, grey cloud with thunder and pouring rain
It tastes like an extra red-hot chilli
It smells like a plate of burnt toast
And it sounds like the roaring thunder
I felt this way when my baby cousin scratched my face!

Nikita Patel (11)
Elsley Primary School, Wembley

Envy

Envy is the colour emerald-green
Envy is like having my soul being sucked out of my body
Envy smells like a bowlful of out of date milk
Envy tastes like a bottle full of sour tears
Envy looks like a beggar looking in a shop window
Envy sounds like someone trying to get through a permanently closed door
I feel envy when no one takes any notice of me.

Daijana Joseph (10)
Elsley Primary School, Wembley

Shyness

Shyness is the colour of baby pink
Shyness feels like the sun shining and smiling at me
Shyness is like when you can't even talk and as if your mouth
                                        is zipped up
Shyness tastes like a sweet candyfloss
Shyness sounds like the birds singing sweetly, early in the morning
Shyness smells like the sweet, unpolluted air
I felt shy when I performed in front of thousands of people.

Arani Ponnambalathasan (11)
Elsley Primary School, Wembley

Lonely

Lonely is purple
It feels like someone's walked away from me
It tastes like dull tuna sandwiches
It smells like a rotten sardine
It looks like a tree stuck in a painting
It sounds like the trees whispering to one another.

Sabrina Saunders (10)
Elsley Primary School, Wembley

Happy

Happy is rainbow coloured
Happy looks like colourful roses
Happy tastes like honey
Happy smells like strawberry ice cream
Happy sounds like people laughing
Happy feels like a soft blanket
I feel happy at school and on my birthday.

Thanusia Veerasingam (11)
Elsley Primary School, Wembley

Angry

The colour of anger is black or dark blue
The feeling of anger is like the world is going to drop on you
The look of anger is like people are all crying
The taste of anger is like eating chilli
The smell of anger is like someone dying
The sound of anger is like a car breaking down in the middle of the
road.

Zhané Thorpe (11)
Elsley Primary School, Wembley

Anxious

Anxious is the colour pink
It feels like splashes of water coming from nowhere
Anxious tastes like fizzy strips running across your tongue
The smell is as if there is suspense in the air
It looks like bubbles bubbling out in excitement
Anxious sounds like popcorn popping eagerly around
I've been anxious when I've waited for a moment to shine.

Ali-Taha Sheikh (11)
Elsley Primary School, Wembley

Dramatic

Dramatic is the colour navy-blue
Rain is what it feels like
Apples is what it tastes like
Mangoes are what it smells like
Lightning is what it looks like
Thunder is what it sounds like
I felt this when a storm attacked the Earth.

Saif Khan (11)
Elsley Primary School, Wembley

Joy

The colour of joy is yellow
Joy feels as soft as a pillow
Joy looks like the beautiful sky
Joy tastes like sweet honey
Joy smells like pretty flowers
Joy sounds like the birds tweeting in the sky
I felt joyful when my baby sister was born.

Kajal Patel (11)
Elsley Primary School, Wembley

Noise

The cry of a child, the thud of a hoof,
The rattle of a snake on my roof,
The sinking of a ship, the shock of a train,
The crunch of a cracker in my vein,
I like noise.

The blow of the wind, the water of the rain,
The pain of the cold in my brain,
The splash of the rain, the squeaking of a mouse,
The knock on a door, in my house
I like noise.

The slamming of the door, the horn of a car,
The tear of paper, the knock on a bar,
The roar of a lion, the bark of a dog,
The ribbit of a frog, near a log,
I like noise.

The shot of a gun, the rattle of a key,
The knock with a spoon, on my cup of tea,
The ring of a phone, the hiss of a snake,
The whoosh of water in a lake,
I like noise.

Nishit Dhanji (11)
Elsley Primary School, Wembley

Happy

Happy is the colour red
It feels like smooth Belgium chocolate
It tastes like soft, creamy hot chocolate
It looks like a flash new Ferrari F50
It smells like sweet, pure honey
It sounds like the calm sea
I felt happy when I got my PlayStation portable before Christmas.

Pritam Parmar (10)
Elsley Primary School, Wembley

Grumpy!

Grumpy is the colour grey
It feels like a hard brick wall not letting me pass
It looks like a puff of smoke filling the room
It tastes like warm ice cream and cotton wool
It smells like someone breaking wind
It sounds like a storm breaking in the clouds
I felt grumpy when I didn't get to go to the Royal Philharmonic
Orchestra in Year 5.

Aniksha Pindoria (10)
Elsley Primary School, Wembley

Angry

Angry is the colour deep, dark red
Angry feels like lava being poured over my head
Angry looks like an earthquake shaking the ground
Angry tastes like hot chilli powder being poured in my mouth
Angry smells like black pepper
Angry sounds like someone jumping on a computer.

Shannon Leigh (10)
Elsley Primary School, Wembley

Peace In The World

Peace in the world is one thing for me
The atmosphere is great!
The leaves, the animals, the trees are important to me
Peace in the world.

Peace in the world is hope for you and me
Because the violence, the wars, the crime is spreading
The nature, the bugs and the bees are important to me
Peace in the world.

Peace in the world is a dream for me
As well as Christians, Muslims, Sikhs and Hindus
The religions and worship are important to me
Peace in the world.

Nikki Tolia (10)
Elsley Primary School, Wembley

Seasons

The winter is near
Snow is falling on the ground
The sun has gone now

The birds are singing
Spring is coming very soon
The daffodils shine

The trees are growing
The temperature is hot
Now that winter has gone.

Abigail Raikes (10)
Keep Hatch Primary School, Wokingham

Lady From Russia

There was a tubby lady from Russia
Who kept on getting blusher
She got trapped in the door
And slipped on the floor
And now she's got a boyfriend called Usher.

Christopher Haggitt (11)
Keep Hatch Primary School, Wokingham

The Beach

The beach is wonderful,
To the naked eye, not special,
The lap of water on our toes
Kids singing songs, philosophical

Deckchairs in stripes,
Of blue, green and red,
Watch the waves,
The only time to rest your head

Put out the picnic mat,
Begin to set up,
Eat your sandy sandwiches
And empty your paper cup

The tide has come in,
Jump the white horses, which lap all around,
See yachts, boats and ships bobbing along,
Spot surfers, they're floating like they only weigh a pound.

Natalie Jackson (11)
Keep Hatch Primary School, Wokingham

What Am I?

I am very good at teaching,
I can win any spelling test,
I know every word in the world,
But you don't find me interesting.
What am I?

Jasmin Cheung (11)
Keep Hatch Primary School, Wokingham

School

S chool is sometimes fun
C lass is really good
H elp is never needed
O pen up the doors
O rchestra play loud songs
L unch is the best!

Jasmine Touchin (11)
Keep Hatch Primary School, Wokingham

What Am I?

I have a cleaning habit
I am sometimes big, long or wide
I am loved by Mum
Dust hates me
Everyone sneezes around me
I am sometimes hairy or furry
I have a plastic spine
I have hair on some of my spine.

Feather duster.

Oliver Wilson (10)
Keep Hatch Primary School, Wokingham

Mrs Crocker

There once was a teacher called Crocker
Who enjoyed a good game of soccer
She ran the school club
Then went down the pub
And had a few shots of Rioja.

Robert Desson (11)
Keep Hatch Primary School, Wokingham

Literacy

L et's get ready for literacy
I t's literacy time
T ime to read a play
E ach and every day
R iddles to learn
A nd a story to tell
C atch up on spellings
Y ell, yell, yell!

Jamie Macdonald (11)
Keep Hatch Primary School, Wokingham

Loose Goose

There's the loose goose,
He's eating chocolate mousse,
Running from shop to shop,
He got a new top,
Smears round his beak,
I heard that door creak.

Loose goose is on the run,
He must be having fun,
Stealing people's shirts and bags,
Even people's smokey fags,
Wearing glasses on his eyes,
It's a good disguise.

A bin bag on his back,
He gave a lady a smack,
Then hid in a bin,
A banana stuck to his chin,
A dog gave him a lick,
Then he was sick!

He went to the loo,
It was just like a zoo,
People everywhere,
All they could do, was stare,
Then they glared
And made the poor loose goose scared.

Jenna Smith (11)
Keep Hatch Primary School, Wokingham

A Cool School Day

Getting out of bed first
Getting dressed that's the worst
Breakfast next, downstairs
Searching in the drawer for pairs.

Cereal pancakes in my tum
It sit down and say, 'Yum, yum!'
Upstairs again to do my hair
I do my teeth to show I care

In the car, *brum, brum*
My bags are packed to learn
School is the next stop
I just feel like I want to flop

Art and literacy are the best
Maths we do east and west
Break and lunch, hip, hip, hooray
And a story to finish the school day

I go home for my tea
My mum, my sis, my friends and me
This is what it is like at my school
It's wicked, but it doesn't rule!

Megan Lee (11)
Keep Hatch Primary School, Wokingham

My Family

My family are cool
To me they rule
You should see my dad
He's good, but mostly bad

My mum's the worst
She moans first
She makes you do things
Which make you burst

My annoying brother Matt
Loves dogs and cats
He also loves cars
And his dream job is a star

My two-year-old brother, Scott
Is cute and loses the plot
He loves Winnie the Pooh
And Tigger too

My grandma is sweet
She's not to beat
She's always there
No matter where

And that's my family
Who are cool
Sometimes they upset me
But they still rule!

Zoe Wood (11)
Keep Hatch Primary School, Wokingham

School

In the morning we sit and read
On our work we all speed
Some people mess about
So they have to go out

At break we go out and play
The teacher always says, 'Do what I say!'
I heard the whistle blow
Off we all go

After break we all come in
Some work went wrong so it's in the bin
We are all getting ready
So we better be steady

Off we go to lunch and play
The teacher always says, 'Do what I say!'
I heard the whistle blow
Off we all go

It's the afternoon
We have to tidy up soon
Doing our work nice and neat
Someone fell off the seat.

Yasmin Castell (11)
Keep Hatch Primary School, Wokingham

What Am I?

I come from the beach
Where children play
And then I get taken away
I get moulded and crushed
They make me into different shapes
Then I am transparent
For everyone to have.

Elliot Atkinson (11)
Keep Hatch Primary School, Wokingham

The Temple

At the temple in the dead of night
The tombs open up
And the dead arise

The glass cracks open
But no one is there
You can't cuddle up with your teddy bear

The moon is starting to peep and shine
When the sun comes out
We can all have a glass of wine.

Felicity Haines (10)
Keep Hatch Primary School, Wokingham

Our Classroom Is Windsor

O ur classroom is neat and tidy
U nderstanding words for literacy
R hyming words for poems

C lean up after we've played
L earning new words
A nd astrology
S ometimes we are allowed to make things
S cience is held on Mondays
R unning and football is on Fridays
O ur lessons are very funny
O ur teacher lets us write in pen
M y teacher is very kind

I ndoor PE is brilliant
S ome of us have the same birthdays

W e love Windsor, it is great
I ndoor break is great
N ow we are having fun
D innertime, we have roast and potatoes
S ome things we do are great
O r sometimes they can be boring
R eally school is OK!

Kasey Smith & Paris Nimako (11)
Keep Hatch Primary School, Wokingham

The Solar System

In space there is the sun,
He lets us have fun!

In space there is Mercury,
He's the planet's Hercules,
In space there is Venus,
Saint of all genius.

In space there is Earth,
Fresh from its birth,
In space there is Mars,
A criminal behind bars.

In space there is Jupiter,
All bold and superior,
In space there is Saturn,
It spins in a pattern.

In space there is Uranus,
Shy unlike Las Vegas,
In space there is Neptune,
It sings with a low tune.

In space there is Pluto,
Like a perfect photo,
The Milky Way
Lets all the planets stay!

Harry Randall & Sami Cengiz (11)
Keep Hatch Primary School, Wokingham

Seasons

Today it is snowing
Yesterday was dry.

Summer rules so dry,
We can go to play, yay!

Winter moves to spring,
Summer comes, hooray!

The grass goes all green
With the sun so bright.

Spring term, warms those hearts
Till autumn comes again.

Children stay up late
Because it's still light.

People sweat
Because the sun's so hot.

School ends for six weeks
And teachers get breaks.

Now back to school
And back to work again.

Ryan James (10)
Keep Hatch Primary School, Wokingham

What Am I?

I am as cheeky as can be
Also really naughty
I have lots of other friends
Also really naughty

We like fruit
We can be big or small
Thin or wide
We like to peel bananas

We like to play all the time
Swinging all the time
We go, 'Ooh aah,'
What am I?

Kirsty Coleman (11)
Keep Hatch Primary School, Wokingham

I Went Back To School

They forgot about me,
They didn't care,
They even went on a trip without me,
They bought a kitten called Jo
And they didn't show me,
They even bought some new swings,
They made me play with clay,
They had a new dinner lady
And I didn't get to say goodbye,
Monday was a horrible day,
But Tuesday was a normal day,
I got to play all day,
I got to play with the kitten
And I didn't have to play with clay,
Tuesday was a lovely day.

Rebekah Haynes (8)
The Silchester Manor School, Taplow

Junk Food Spell!

A cheese and onion packet of crisps,
Mixed with apple pips,
Add a cut-up slice of pizza,
Make sure it's margherita.

Luke Battson (10)
The Silchester Manor School, Taplow

My Spell

The fallen angels hidden lies,
The powdered dust up in skies,
A sprinkle of times last power,
The Devil smiles in every hour,
An iron wolf's rotting insides,
Devil's grin and lions' hides,
The gentle unicorn's beating heart,
Snakes, long dead, come in a cart,
Sea's froth, dragon's horn,
Ghost baby, ten years after being born,
A bat's scaly claw,
Riding Devil, breaking law,
Hair of fish, blue whale's teeth,
Gentle shark drowned on a reef,
Eye of death, chip of moon,
Crazy bear which will come soon.

Karla Berglund (11)
The Silchester Manor School, Taplow

Hopis

Once an annoying, mysterious creature lived,
Once it cried with the sorrow of its heart,
Once it slowly walked from a cold-hearted family,
Once it lay under a branched, dark tree,
Once it had to live on nothing,
Once it never saw the light of day.
Hopis.

Courtney Mallon (11)
The Silchester Manor School, Taplow

Bats

I like bats,
They fly at midnight,
They sleep in the morning
And wake at night,
They fly very fast
And live in caves,
They sleep upside down
And are very brave,
They come at Hallowe'en
And children get very scared,
Their eyes are yellow
And give you a frightening glare.

Ismaeel Malik (9)
The Silchester Manor School, Taplow

Winter

Slippery snow flutters slowly onto the wet and muddy grass,
Leafless trees freeze madly swaying one side to another,
The breezy wind rushes strongly and swiftly,
Children build snowmen in the wintertime snow,
Snowmen stare coldly at the people inside,
Wet sheets of rain sprinkling down heavily and quickly,
Birds hibernate and look after their young,
Freezing grass is covered with ice and whiteness,
Beautiful stars hang in the sky shining like beautiful angels
dancing around.

Faizah Ahmed (8)
The Silchester Manor School, Taplow

Sunflowers Shining

S pecial flowers shine in your garden
U nder the summer sun
N ew and bright
F lowers dance in the light
L ook at the brown centre
O h, look at all those seeds
W hirling round and round
E very summer the sunflower comes out to grow in the sun
R ound and round the garden we go with the sunflower
                                        growing so tall.

Daniel Ross (7)
Winbury School, Maidenhead

Harvest Recipe

Take very black berries from the bush,
Orange crunchy carrots from the ground
And tall wheat that stands golden in the field
Add nuts that are brown,
Oranges from the bowl
And juicy blueberries from the shop.

Mix in purple cherries as dark as silk,
Crunchy lettuce that rabbits like to eat
And marrows growing fat.

Decorate with autumn leaves, yellow and red,
Grapes hanging on vines
And dewy grass in the morning,
Harvest is a sharing time of year.

Jarod Hind (7)
Winbury School, Maidenhead

Near And Far

Here I am, look at me,
Did you know I was stung by a bee?

Quite near to me there is a very big hill,
I will climb it tomorrow, yes I will!

Further away is Legoland,
Inside I can hear the band!

A long way off in Italy,
There are lots of lovely things to see.

In Africa there is a lot of sand,
It is a big, distant land.

Far away in space is Mars
And there are millions of stars.

Jack Tooley (7)
Winbury School, Maidenhead

Sunflowers

S unflowers are special flowers
U nder the sky there are some beautiful sunflowers
N ow I am growing some sunflowers
F lowers yellow and blazing and bright
L ovely sunflowers in the sun
O h, lovely sunflowers I hope you will bring the sun today
W e all love sunflowers
E very time I see a sunflower it makes me smile
R ain on the sunflowers so it grows.

William Swift (7)
Winbury School, Maidenhead

Poppies For Remembrance

P oppies are very pretty on the grass
O ver the fields are lots of poppies, like a sea of red
P recious poppies waving around
P apery petals like tissue pictures
I wear my poppy with pride
E ach November we remember
S ing a song about poppies.

Rebecca Swift (7)
Winbury School, Maidenhead

Penguin Parade

Ten silly penguins skiing through the snow
One is called Billy and look at him go!

Nine crazy penguins standing upside down
One fell over like a clown!

Eight mad penguins driving racing cars
Zooming around like superstars!

Seven groovy penguins dancing in the snow
One lost his partner so he had to go!

Six sad penguins trudging through the storm
Wanting their supper so they could keep warm.

Five fit penguins running all around
One stopped and heard a sound.

Four funny penguins telling silly jokes
One of them told a naughty hoax!

Three funky penguins in a fashion show
One was disqualified so he had to bow and go!

Two tired penguins having a feast
One burst 'cause he ate too much yeast.

One lonely penguin staring at the sky
He was sad so he had to cry!

Jonathan Cameron (8)
Winbury School, Maidenhead

Near And Far

Look at me with my fair hair
It's very hard to sit on my chair!

Quite near to my house is Holyport Hall
Sometimes we can play ball.

Further away we can play on the sand
England is a beautiful land.

A long way off is a country called Spain
There is not a lot of rain.

Very far away Iceland is cold
The polar bears are very bold!

In outer space it is very, very far away
Down below it is such a beautiful day.

Emma Delgado (7)
Winbury School, Maidenhead

Poppies For Remembrance

P retty poppies in the field
O ut comes the sun and breeze and the poppies sway in the sun
P oppies' petals crumble very easily like tissue paper
P opular flowers which are very pretty
I mportant to remember soldiers and wear a poppy
E ach and every poppy in the field is special
S ing a song that your daddy is home from the war.

Abigail Leone (8)
Winbury School, Maidenhead

Penguin Fun

Ten friendly penguins skating on the ice
Wiggling and jiggling, looking very nice.

Nine little penguins playing in the snow
Dodging snowballs as they go!

Eight jolly penguins going for a ride
Some of them needed a guide.

Seven hungry penguins wanting their fish
Diving to look, with a swish!

Six sleepy penguins wanting to go to bed
Because they had hurt their heads.

Five noisy penguins making such a din
Having a competition to see who will win!

Four cute penguin babies having such fun
Some of their mums called them for a bun.

Three floppy penguins going fishing in a hole
All they found was an old shoe sole!

Two smiley penguins playing with each other
Their mother called them to help their brother.

One lonely penguin looking for his friends
He found them all and that's
The end!

Riya Bhatia (7)
Winbury School, Maidenhead

Penguin Countdown

Ten funny penguins on a washing line
One jumped in the water so there were nine.

Nine hungry penguins having fish on a plate
One was sick so there were eight!

Eight dreamy penguins thinking about Heaven
One went to sleep so there were seven.

Seven cheerful penguins listening to tricks
One got bored so there were six.

Six happy penguins glad to be alive
One went fishing so there were five.

Five tired penguins fixing a door
One went home so there were four.

Four starving penguins eating their tea
One was never hungry so there were three.

Three quiet penguins they had the flu
One got better so there were two.

Two happy penguins in Hong Kong
One went shopping so there was one.

One lonely penguin staring at the sky
Waving at his friends and saying
Goodbye!

Laura Anne Barnes (8)
Winbury School, Maidenhead